APOTHEOSIS

BY IAN J. MARTIN

Seiders House Publishing
P. O. Box 4341
West Richland Washington 99353

Dedicated to a fish, a bug, an owl, and a kitten.

E

CHAPTER I (№Æ) CATHARSIS

CHAPTER II (№∫∂) KENOSIS

CHAPTER III (№∆) GNOSIS

0

Uncertainty

The feeling of a puzzle piece that never quite aligns,
Going through the motions blindly, trailing off behind.
The foundation that we've settled on is smeared and blurred by rain,
The edges double, then refocus, time and time again.

My lifeline's gone slack,
I'll never find my way back.

Uncertainty, uneasiness, that sinking feeling I know best,
It finds its way unbidden and groping to the chest,
It's never simple as the things easiest to fix,
Not fight or flight, but stand perplexed, waiting for the trick.

There has to be a way away somewhere along this road,
Uncertainty has led me here, tired and alone.

There has to be a way away, the path was here, I know.
Uncertainty has led me here, so lost, and yet…. I'm home.

White static snow on black.
So begins the journey back.

SPhangingACE

Alert.
Alert.
Klaxons wail.
Shields are down,
Life support's failed.

Which way is up? What's right from wrong?
What is this place? Do I belong?
The laws of physics as we know them exist to be shattered,
Like preconceived notions any of it mattered.

Warning.
Warning.
Strobes blink slow.
Overwhelmed and draining down,
With light-years left to go.

Which way is up? What's right from wrong?
What is this place? Do I belong?
The laws of physics as we know them exist to be shattered,
Like preconceived notions any of it mattered.

The monolith is looming massive, silent and serene,
The signal fades to static on the screen.
Am I alone now?
Am I alone?
I can't see where I am, drifting far from home.

Like a Circle

I always said I'd do the things that you loved to do.
I never took the time to ask what that meant to you.
I only gave away the husk, an empty shell that fades to dust,
My curtain's drawn; I fade to black.

"Like a circle,"
She said.
Little voices echoing, reverberating in my head,
"Will never end,"
She said.
The halfway point - alive and dead.

Is it just my presence in the room?
That makes you feel like chanting doom?
Pound on the drums, say, "Kāli-ma,"
Extract the heart and close the tomb?

"Like a circle,"
Unbroken.
Little voices breaking down the walls,
"Will never end,"
Unspoken.
I'm frozen up, my engine stalls.

The circle breaks and then reforms,
The standards settle all for something less
Than what there was before.
Or is it more?

Iceman Cometh

It took some time to realize,
That these walls have ears and eyes.
The words I hurl to great effect,
Amplify, turn and reflect.

"I've got tone," the speaker cracks,
The chaff's away, bank and attack.
I drop the bomb and roll away,
Hiroshima, meet Enola Gay.

That magnificent display of all my power and might,
Accomplished very little, aside from embers in the night.
Aside perhaps, I think, from the shadows burnt on walls,
And now the pilot asks himself: Was it really worth it all?

And in the utter devastation,
Midst phantoms of the lost,
Crisp and silent desolation,
To the victor goes the cost.

To the victor goes the cost.

Daylight?

Cut left through the jog in the tunnel,
Head straight through the junction and stay.
There's a light at the end of this passage,
I feel a breeze and I'm longing to say:

Has it been worth the wait?
I know it has for me.
Is it worth the pain?
I guess we'll wait and see.
What I knew, and what I felt, while I was trapped down in the dark,
Is what you know, what you feel, when I won't open up my heart.

I got turned around down here,
The twists and turns ensnared my brain.
The light at the end of the passage,
Was just a dying candle's flame.

Has it been worth the wait?
I know it has for me.
Is it worth the pain?
I guess we'll wait and see.
What I knew, and what I felt, while I was trapped down in the dark,
Is what you know, what you feel, when I won't open up my heart.

Lost in this endless labyrinth,
I swear someday I'll make it out.
I don't want you to wait for me,
Filled with uncertainty and doubt.

Mr. False Shepherd †

"I'll make this simple," said the man with the beard.
"Heed my words, or this gets really weird."
He said it calmly, convinced to stand his ground.
But he shook when he saw that no one came around.

Shout at the skies and stamp your feet,
Mr. False Shepherd,
Haven't you heard the end is here?
Preach it brother.
Buy up stock in sandwich boards,
Mr. Fatalistic.
Let's try to be more realistic.
Doot doot da doo da doo da doo.

"The world is coming to an end!" the man emphatically declares,
He wants to know why you don't care.
This man's afraid of letting go,
Of all the things he doesn't know,
Oh, lord, he wants you scared.

Shout at the skies and stamp your feet,
Mr. False Shepherd,
Haven't you heard the end is here?
Preach it brother.
Buy up stock in sandwich boards,
Mr. Fatalistic.
Let's try to be more realistic.
Doot doot da doo da doo da doo.

Perhaps a little soft-shoe, along with the spittle on your lip,
Would serve to get your point across, but will it silence your critics?

Shout at the skies and stamp your feet,
Mr. False Shepherd,
Now we know the end is here,
Preach it brother.
Go out and paint those sandwich boards,
Mr. Fatalistic.
Let's try to be more realistic.
Doot doot da doo da doo da doo.

Nothing Rhymes for No Reason

Black, a stack,
Of wreckage charred and burned.
Relax, attack,
Perhaps someday we'll learn.
Step back, gone slack,
It's someone else's turn.
The tact, I lack,
My eyes begin to burn.

Where have you gone?
Princesses of Rhyme and Reason,
Left us to fend for ourselves,
Curators of this living Hell.

Exact revenge,
On me for my sins.
My fate is sealed,
Before this all begins.
Plunge deep and twist,
The knife into my heart.
And let me die,
Before this even starts.

Where have you gone?
Princesses of Rhyme and Reason,
Left us to fend for ourselves,
Curators of this living Hell.

Retread my steps,
Backwards at half-pace.
Retrace the lines,
That led us to this place.
Replay the scene,
The way we've set the tone.
Reset the game,
Let's try another round.

The Shoal †

What happens when the lights go out,
Is a great and secret show.
Bask in the signs and marquee lights,
Prepare for the unknown.
The spectacle, the sights and sounds,
The banners now unfurl,
With showmanship and theatrics,
Foreign to this world.

See the man without a head,
How could it be that he's not dead?
The woman there, with golden locks,
She reads your mind, but never talks.
This charming fellow by my side,
Has never failed and never tried.
And lastly, you, with face aglow,
Welcome to our humble show.

What happens when the lights go out,
Is a great and secret show.
Bask in the signs and marquee lights,
Prepare for the unknown.
The spectacle, the sights and sounds,
The banners now unfurl,
With showmanship and theatrics,
Foreign to this world.

And now it greatly pleases me,
(Something that is rarely seen)
To bring to you our vetted host,
The one that you've demanded most.
Now dim the lights and hush the crowd.
No one dare to make a sound.
Before you now upon the stage,
I give you, man, consumed by rage.

What happens when the lights go out,
Is a great and secret show.
Bask in the signs and marquee lights,
Prepare for the unknown.
The spectacle, the sights and sounds,
The banners now unfurl,
With showmanship and theatrics,
Foreign to this world.

Kraken

Across a calm and serene sea,
Not a gull, nor angel cries.
No signs of life pollute the scene,
A soft breeze gently sighs.
But 'neath the waves, a shadow stirs,
Sliding through the depths.
This monstrous beast of legend-borne,
Awaits to steal my breath.

The sky grows dark and clouds roll in,
Thunder cracks and peals.
The once-still surface of my soul,
Roils and then reveals...

What fresh hell hath thou wrought,
By awakening from slumber,
This raging, giant, wrathful thing,
Which had been held encumbered?
I could have stayed its hand before;
Undone this misery,
But now the Devil is unleashed,
And I've no sympathy.

As the masts collapse and split,
The forecastle's rent asunder,
A smile plays across my lips,
And I let myself slip under…

Beneath the calm and serene sea,
Not a gull, nor angel cries.
No signs of life pollute the scene,
The light begins to die.
Into the void, commit this soul,
Repent for all your sins,
Abandon hope, all ye who enter,
Its fury never ends.

The Eye of the Storm †

If you count the beats,
You'll find your way home.
If you follow your heart,
I swear you won't be alone.
Have faith that pure love,
Will always avail.
Please take my hand,
And push on through the gale.

Only once you've traveled through,
The darkest hours of this night,
Is it possible to make your peace,
And turn to face the light.
Fear not the raging deluge,
Nor the stinging shards of glass.
Take solace simply knowing,
That someday, this too, shall pass.

Together we stand,
As the world tears apart,
On this sliver of earth,
Both pierced through the heart.
We feign resolution,
Both drenched to the bone.
Yet we've struggled on,
And found our way home.

The ground finally gives way,
We huddle exposed.
You've weathered such torment,
I've hidden in prose.
With apparent relief,
Yet a hint of dismay,
The demons we've faced,
Retreat from the day.

I'll always remember,
The endless night in the field,
When the world was ending,
Yet we refused to yield.
For though the earth crumbled,
And our lives lost their form,
We found a safe place,
In the eye of the storm.

Faith, or Lack Thereof

Fear the faithless,
As you fear God,
For they've nothing left to lose.

Fear the joyful,
As you fear me,
For I've nothing left to prove.

Be afraid, it's comforting,
Familiar, rending claws,
You've lost the will to carry on,
Have faith in all your flaws.

Fear the darkness,
As you fear hope,
Seek your solace any way.

Fear the light,
As you fear yourself,
Take refuge from the day.

Be afraid, it's comforting,
Familiar, rending claws,
You've lost the will to save yourself,
Have faith in all your flaws.

Self-Immolation †

This must be done to prove a point,
I cannot make alone.
I steel myself, prepare the match,
Of pyrophoric stone.
Anoint myself from head to foot, and heave a somber breath,
I've heard that fire cleanses, and to pray for a swift death.

Bitter, white-hot agony crawls upon my flesh.
The flames completely penetrate, searing through my breast.
I've found my place amongst the stars, burning in the sky,
Their luminescent brilliance shining long after they die.

In utter silence, my statement made,
The fire begins to gutter.
The people gasp, and turn away,
And some are heard to mutter:
"So sad, it is, that this poor man,
Could never find his place.
Alas, it seems the point is lost,
This life has been a waste."

The clouds move in, the Earth un-phased,
The people shuffle on.
I've left this world a better place,

Now that I am gone.

Questions

Do I frighten you?
No need respond, it's on your face,
Written plain as day.

I question, "Why, what have I done?
Am I a monster or a man?"
This scarred and twisted visage,
Only wants to hold your hand.
"Is that too much to ask?" I ponder,
The solution's never clear.
Is it possible to win the heart,
Of one consumed by fear?

Do I frighten you?
No need respond, it's on your face,
Written plain as day.

My presumption of simplicity,
Makes it an easy task,
To lurk within the shadows,
Hiding behind a mask.
The man behind the monster,
That you've come to know and loathe,
Is still a man, when's said and done,
And all he wants is love.

Do I frighten you?
No need respond, it's on your face,
Written plain as day.

Dimorphism †

Take in the sights around you,
As quickly as you're able,
Things aren't always what they seem,
Reality's unstable.
What once was very simple,
Taken plainly as a fact,
Dissolves into the ether,
When we find something it lacks.
Now, this theory that I took to heart,
Both a blessing and a boon,
Becomes something of an albatross,
And begins to make me swoon.
Perception is reality,
Though what I perceive is lost;
Knowledge is my burden,
Upon my back a cross.
Recollect, now, if you can,
All that was said before,
The things I knew, that were so real,
Simply are not any more.

Eager

Can I? Can I?
Not until you grow.
Will I? Will I?
You may never know.
Do I? Do I?
Try to take it slow.
Have I? Have I?
The answer is still no.

Can you? Can you?
I haven't ever tried.
Will you? Will you?
That part of me has died.
Do you? Do you?
I will not tell a lie.
Have you? Have you?
I don't want to make you cry.

Could I? Could I?
You absolutely should.
Would I? Would I?
It's only for your good.
Should I? Should I?
I only know, I would.
May I? May I?
If only that you could.

Could you? Could you?
I think it's best I do.
Would you? Would you?
I did this all for you.
Should you? Should you?
I've made myself the fool.
These things I do, all to please you,
Oh, how I wish that they weren't true.

11:07

I sit

&

Contemplate

Existence

Wondering

Idly

What it means

Freezing

Climate controlled

Squinting

@

Two screens

Perhaps there's nothing more

-a sigh-

A case of:

Too-Little™

Too-Late™

&

Now

To my elation

The

Time

Is

Now

11:08

Maybe?

In my few short years, I've seen some things,
I'd much rather forget.
And while you may not think that much,
I've had to live through it.
I've spanned the gaps, gained and lost faith,
Developed my own views.
Had heartache, joy, and bitterness,
And wept over bad news.
One thing life has made me ask,
Often late at night,
Is whether there exists a God,
Of purity and light?
This loaded question earns a man,
An ounce or two of shame,
But I know you've asked these questions,
For inside we're all the same.
And now I will elucidate,
My stance on the issue:
If there truly is a God,
Would He care whether we knew?

Proof †

I see one side of the situation,
Though I know more must exist.
Torn apart by infatuation,
I still let myself persist.
I often hear 'masochism',
Flung about my ears.
Filling the yawning schism,
Between my desires and my fears.

Why do the things I yearn for
Result in so much pain?
Do I enjoy the suffering?
What do I have to gain?
Why is there such a longing;
This willingness to ache?
It seems my soul's the happiest,
When my heart begins to break.

And so, again, the path here splits;
An unbalanced equation.
I rest, and ponder as I sit,
Open to persuasion.
Do I choose the road unknown
In hopes it leads to you?
Or best that I forge on alone,
In pursuit of something new?

Without much pomp and circumstance,
No hint of fanfare found,
I finally choose to take a chance,
And push up off the ground.
Ahead of me these paths diverge,
But both lead to certain fate,
Where pain and pleasure can converge,
And both can satiate.

My decision made, I start to move,
Bolstered-up with pride.
And though it may seem odd to some,
The pain proves I'm alive.

Balance

Ask yourself this simple question:
Is it worth the cost?
Tumbling down the rabbit hole,
Disorientated and lost.
Much like little Alice,
Awash in Wonderland,
Not everything is rational,
But everything is planned.

When you've finally landed,
And stand on your own feet,
Prepare your reparations,
For the people that you meet.
For there are consequences,
The Devil's owed his due.
Has the debt upon your soul,
Been worth the price to you?

If you can face this question,
Nod your head and smile,
We'll know the soul inside you,
Has been dead for quite a while.
For in the end, the scales balance,
And no matter what you've weathered,
A heart full of spite and misery,
Always outweighs a feather.

Always

Sometimes I have to laugh,
And turn my face away,
When I hear the irony,
In the words you say.

Sometimes I have to lie,
And wish I'd told the truth,
When I have the answer,
But can't provide the proof.

Sometimes I become angry,
And have to grit my teeth,
When your actions fall,
Far beyond belief.

Sometimes I have to cower,
And cover up my ears,
When your words hit close to home,
And prey upon my fears.

Sometimes I have to run,
And find a place to hide,
When I feel you've found a way,
To see who I am inside.

Catharsis

Free me from this prison,
Of grief, suffering, and shame.
Exorcise the demons that have long inflicted such pain.

Catharsis, cathartic words,
Bleeding on the page.
Catharsis, cathartic words,
Shattering this cage.
Catharsis is the way I deal,
The way that I survive.
Catharsis is the way I feel,
It brings me back to life.

Clear away the storm clouds,
That rained on fertile ground.
In the sodden earth, it seems that new life can be found.

Catharsis, cathartic words,
Bleeding on the page.
Catharsis, cathartic words,
Shattering this cage.
Catharsis is the way I deal,
The way that I survive.
Catharsis is the way I feel,
It brings me back to life.

Don't run,
Don't hide,
Embrace the memory,
It's done,
I'm fine,
There's so much left to be.

Catharsis, cathartic words,
Bleeding on the page.
Catharsis, cathartic words,
Shattering this cage.
Catharsis is the way I deal,
The way that I survive.
Catharsis is the way I feel,
It brings me back to life.

Fear Not

Stop there,
You're alright – Just breathe
Don't run away,
You don't owe them a thing.

I'm here,
Open your eyes – Just see
Quit trying to hide,
And just be.

Fear not,
The little voice inside you screams
Hear me,
I'm right by your side
And will continue to be,
Fear not,
The little girl inside you dreams
Hear me,
I'm right by your side,
And will continue to be.

Stand tall,
You're golden – I see
You for your light,
You don't owe me a thing.

I'm here,
Don't hesitate – Be free
Quit trying to hide,
And just be.

Fear not,
The little voice inside you screams
Hear me,
I'm right by your side
And will continue to be,
Fear not,
The little girl inside you dreams
Hear me,
I'm right by your side,
And will continue to be.

I'm here,
Don't hesitate – Be free
Quit trying to hide,
And just be.
Just be.

Pieces

Little bits fly
Shards of the past
Broken and dazzling
Pieces of glass

Time seems to slow
Reflections ingrained
Fragments dispersing
Falling like rain

The mirror is cracked
Shattered apart
Scattered like ashes
Pieces of my heart

Easy as Pi †

This is the ultimate, this is the pinnacle,
This is the apex; a fucking miracle.
It's been a long while in the making.
Now it's high-time for the taking.

That golden ring is within my grasp,
My time to shine (and then relapse),
The carousel of life completes its revolutions.
The wooden creatures slow and still,
And I am finally moved by will,
To undertake dramatic evolution.

At the vertex of this parabola,
I had a theory, and soon a formula.
If you subtract and then divide,
The sole remainder is what's inside.

That golden ring is within my grasp,
My time to shine (and then relapse),
The carousel of life completes its revolutions.
The wooden creatures slow and still,
And I am finally moved by will,
To undertake dramatic evolution.

Here I am again; the cycle repeats.
Will I ever win? Or suffer more defeat?
Sad to say, I'll see you next time friends,
This fractal spiral never ends.

Battle Lines and Modern Times †

After a time, the dust will settle,
That long clouded my sight.
Another empty test of mettle,
Of courageousness and might.
My heart grows weary of the strife,
I often scream in vain,
Searching for purpose in life,
To justify this pain.

Choose your side,
Head or tails,
No one wins,
We all fail.
Pick your battles,
Lines are drawn.
What's the point?
I can't go on.

Give me something, anything,
To save me from myself.
The empty voids of loneliness,
Replace the fires of Hell.
And in this dark, I weep alone,
Ashamed of what I am:
Animated flesh and bone,
A mockery of man.

Either side,
Head or tails,
No one won,
We all failed.
The battle's fought,
The lines were drawn,
There was no point,
Yet I go on.

On the blood-soaked earth I lay,
Gazing sightless toward the sky,
My very soul exposed and flayed,
I long simply to die.
The sun peers out and warms my face,
Cool rain begins to pour,
I've reached my final resting place,
I won't struggle any more.

Homicide Pact

Laugh it up, you mother fucker,
I hope you get your due.
If only I could be the one,
I'd put an end to you.
I'd make it slow and torturous,
Ensure you beg and plead,
Twisting the blade, so satisfied,
Is exactly what I need.

There are some people in this world,
Who don't deserve to be.
I can see from your expression,
That you don't agree with me.
If you could feel the pain you've wrought,
The innocence that you've consumed,
You'd pray for me to finish this,
To bleed the life from you.

But lucky you, you've fooled them all.
I applaud you for your skill,
Standing silent, just off stage,
Waiting for my kill.
As the curtains close,
And you take your final bow,
I stab the knife into your gut,
Whispering, "Who's laughing now?"

Numb

I can't feel anything anymore,
And that's alright with me.
I don't need to hear your voice,
And I don't need to see.
I've let my limbs go dead and limp,
I've left my mind to roam.
The numbness settles in again;
I finally feel at home.

Spike the vein with anesthetic,
Give me what I need.
Open up another bottle,
Pour it into me.
I don't want this anymore,
But it's not my choice to make,
This self-sustaining misery,
Dictates which path I take.

Free me, please free me.
This is not who I am.
Help me, please help me.
I can't do this again.

But I'm numb.

Numb.

Agony and Irony

I finally got the joke last night,
Staring in the dark.
Straining for coherence,
The lines becoming stark.
I finally got the joke last night.
It hurt to see the truth.
To open up my eyes at last,
And see the blinding proof.

Agony and Irony
Collide
What makes it ache also makes it sweet
Agony and Irony
Inside
Victory from suffering defeat

I finally got the joke today,
Feeling quite ashamed.
I took too long grasping at straws,
Shuffling the blame.
I finally got the joke today,
You told me years ago.
It didn't make much sense back then,
Now I wish I didn't know.

Agony and Irony
Collide
What makes it ache also makes it sweet
Agony and Irony
Inside
Victory from suffering defeat

Agony and Irony
Collide
What makes it ache also makes it sweet
Agony and Irony
Inside
Victory from suffering defeat

Objectivity

This is the epicenter,
The origin.
No chance to reconsider,
So it begins.

Back, back, back,
I'll take it all back (*I'm taken aback*)
For the chance to make it right.
Back, back, back,
I'd take it all back (*I'm taken aback*)
If I could end this all tonight.

I told you one thing,
You must have heard another.
Why are we fighting,
When we could save each other?

Back, back, back,
I'll take it all back (*I'm taken aback*)
For the chance to make it right.
Back, back, back,
I'd take it all back (*I'm taken aback*)
If I could end it all tonight.

Take it back, just take it back.
Take it back, just take it back.
Take it back, just take it back.
Take it back, just take it all back, again.

Who Are You Now?

Who are you now that the spotlight has faded?
Who are you now that you're broken and jaded?
All your sycophants have denounced your name,
Dashing what hope you had left in the game.

Who are you now that your limelight has passed?
Who are you now the foundation's collapsed?
What hasn't been stolen or rotted apart,
Was mothballed and crated alongside your heart.

Who are you now that the curtains are drawn?
Who are you now that you don't belong?
The life that you lead is ever a lie,
Now we know who you are, but we still wonder

Why?

For Now †

Everything is beautiful.
I've finally reached a clearing.
The air is so pure now.
I can hear the birds singing.

For now,
Things have reached balance.
For now,
I've found a place to call home.
For now,
I can dream of a future.
For now,
I don't feel alone.

I've seen this place before,
Tasted it in dreams.
Never thought I'd live it,
Unreal as it seems.

For now,
I can settle at ease.
For now,
We've reached armistice.
For now,
The hatchets are buried.
For now,
I'm happy with this.

Someday this will end.
Why bother to ponder?
Our lives are just streams;
We meander and wander.

For now,
Things have reached balance.
For now,
I've found a place to call home.
For now,
I can dream of a future.
For now,
I don't feel alone.

Random Encounter

In a random encounter,
A meeting of the minds,
The fictions I've written,
Begin to unwind.
It's once in a lifetime;
This chance to be,
Accepted and loved,
Only…
For me.

Down the long road,
Twenty-seven years deep, now.
Where have you been?
What, why, when, and how?

Dear God, how'd I survive?
I was barely alive.

In a random encounter,
A meeting of the minds,
The fictions I've written,
Begin to unwind.
It's once in a lifetime;
This chance to be,
Accepted and loved,
Only…
For me.

What do we do now?
The lanes are all open,
The lights have turned green,
And here's what I'm hoping:

You'll stay here by my side,
'til the end of the line.

In a random encounter,
A meeting of the minds,
The fictions I've written,
Begin to unwind.
It's once in a lifetime;
This chance to be,
Accepted and loved,
Only…
For me.

Do What You Can ƒ

Take a chance for once in your life,
Step off the ledge and fly.
You're only defeating yourself this time;
I know that it hurts you to try.
Take your hands off the wheel for a moment,
Let yourself feel the road.
There are miles of highway laid out before you,
But you don't have to face it alone.

Like the worst idea;
The greatest disaster.
Shake off the reigns and become your own master.
Welcome to your life – Do what you can.
It's terrifying;
So liberating.
In this moment, it's all for the taking.
Welcome to your life – Do what you can.

Take a chance to be something greater,
Imagine yourself as the king.
And never you mind the knaves or the jesters,
Bouncing around in the ring.
Give yourself the time you need,
There's an infinite supply.
You've spent a lifetime laying-low,
But now's the time to try.

Like the worst idea;
The greatest disaster.
Shake off the reigns and become your own master.
Welcome to your life – Do what you can.
It's terrifying;
So liberating.
In this moment, it's all for the taking.
Welcome to your life – Do what you can.

It's time to try again.
It's time to come alive.
It's time to love again.
It's time to be alright.

I Guess I Was Wrong (Big Surprise) †

I guess I was wrong,
Not for the first time.
I guess I screwed up,
Somewhere 'long the line.
I guess I'll move on,
Like ol' David Banner.
I guess this is so long,
Don't act like it mattered.

And what a big surprise,
I never saw coming.
Yet it seems I've told a lie,
So it's best I stick with humming.

I guess I was wrong,
Not for the first time.
I guess I screwed up,
Somewhere 'long the line.
I guess I'll move on,
Like ol' David Banner.
I guess this is so long,
Don't act like it mattered.

It's a matter of perspective,
Whether I'm right or you're wrong.
For me the hardest part is,
You've known all along.

I should have held myself back,
Anticipation at bay,
But the train has jumped its tracks,
And as much as it hurts me to say:

I guess I was wrong,
It wasn't the first time.
I know I'll screw up,
Again down the line.
And then I'll move on,
Like ol' David Banner.
And then it's so long,
'cause none of it mattered.

Definite Misfit †

You're a definite misfit,
But not a lost cause.
Been stuck in the middle,
Eternally lost.
You cry and you struggle,
When you're all alone,
But when the world watches,
You're as if hewn from stone.

Whatever happened to giving a shit?
Remember that time when you swore not to quit?
Some time I know that you'll deal with it,
But 'til that day comes, you're a definite misfit.

You're a definite misfit,
Believe me, I know.
Every time that you misstep,
Time seems to slow.
I tried so hard to save you,
But you just pulled me down,
Gasping for air,
Until we'd both drowned.

Whatever happened to giving a shit?
Remember that time when you swore not to quit?
Some time I know that you'll deal with it,
But 'til that day comes, you're a definite misfit.

You're a definite misfit,
Born just to go bad.
Now that you're behind me,
I'm wistfully glad.
I know one day you'll find them,
The answers that fit,
But 'til that day comes,
You're a definite misfit.

Compulsion

The light shines out,
The opened door,
I see my dozen friends.
I pick my poison,
First one, then more,
Praying that this ends.

The fizzle-pop,
A twist off top,
Excites the beast in me.
Barley and hops,
Why can't I stop?
I wish I could be free.

Compelled,
Unwilling,
Break the cycle, please.
Unwell,
It's killing,
What left I had of me.

Drained last dregs,
Of dead soldiers,
Littering the floor.
On my last legs,
Though feeling bolder,
I fight the thirst for more.

Compelled,
Unwilling,
Break the cycle, please.
Unwell,
It's killing,
What left I had of me.

Unfinished †

Let me pose this question,
About the nature of our lives.
The quest for absolution;
The things for which we strive.
Why long for integration,
Yet quail from the embrace?
Illusory, ephemeral;
Phantoms in this place.

We're all unfinished sculptures,
Hewn from clay and dust.
We struggle to complete ourselves,
Doing what we may and must.
Like the fair Venus de Milo,
Incomplete, yet still divine,
Our beauty is our brokenness:
Each flaw truly sublime.

Disposable Muses

My disposable muses,
Often blow their fuses,
And turn on their maestro in spite.
They've suffered abuses,
But still have their uses,
At times when the mood feels just right.

Damaged by fire,
Acting haywire,
They stutter and sputter and wheeze.
Filled up with ire,
They call me a liar,
Blindly refusing to cease.

They function as teachers,
These ungodly preachers;
The pain they inflict breaks my heart.
These expendable creatures,
With similar features,
All provide fuel for my art.

What?

Did I miss something here?
What exactly just happened?
The steam roller's in gear,
I think I've been flattened.
Last I checked, things were fine,
Then they all went to hell.
It seems that crossing the line,
Is now all fine and well.

Pack up the butcher knives, let's agree to disagree.
Thus far, from my perspective, life's been good to me.
I don't know the right way for me to make you see,
Stop spitting vitriolic hate, and just let yourself be free.

Well, I've let my guard down,
(Bad idea, so let's move on.)
I can see things as they are now,
The ugly duckling ain't a swan.
My white-knight complex's getting old,
I'm out of words to hurl.
I'll reiterate what you've been told:
Stop fighting against the world.

Pack up the butcher knives, let's agree to disagree.
Thus far, I've done all I can just to leave you be.
I still don't know the right way for me to make you see,
Stop trying to eradicate and just let yourself be free.

So much anger, so much hate,
It brings such suffering.
As much too little, as too late,
It brings me to my knees.
Look at my hands; they're full of baubles,
Gathered up for you.
I'm left with a world of troubles,
But it's the best that I can do.

Will o' the Wistful

Welcome to a sad song about finding happiness,
In the most unusual places.
The names and the faces,
Have been changed to avoid undue duress.

Always so gloomy and gloriously downtrodden,
I've been beaten down and walked upon.
I've waited for so long,
For the promise of the silver lining.

There's nothing wrong with finding time to smile,
Though, Lord knows for me it's been a while.

You're so happy all the time,
It only makes me want to cry.
Who am I? What does this all mean?
What's my motivation in this scene?
To you, I'm words heaped in a pile,
Lacking substance, missing style.

It's finally come time to shift to a new perspective;
At last to change my jaded outlook.
Perhaps to close the book.
Turn critical towards the introspective.

These grand expectations are truly my undoing,
A sad truth a wise man once told me.
Now I think I can see.
Release this existence I've been ruing.

CHAPTER II
(№∫ə)
KENOSIS

Pace Yourself

Ease up, kid
You've only just begun,
Slow down,
Walk before you run.

Restraint's never been your strong suit,
Throw caution to the wind,
Forget all that came before this,
And how that story ends.
Perhaps this time will differ,
You plead with tired eyes,
But your spirit's reached its limit,
Evaporating with a sigh.

Ease up, kid
Take a moment, take a breath,
Coming in first,
Only wins an early death.

Restraint's never been your strong suit,
Throw caution to the wind,
Forget what came before this,
And how that story ends.
Perhaps this time will differ,
You plead with tired eyes,
But your spirit's reached its limit,
Evaporating with a sigh.

Something Different

It's time for change;
Strike the set;
A change of pace;
Try to forget.
All of this becomes so wrote and stale.

Revitalize;
Clear the stage;
Reset the scene;
Look with fresh eyes.
Tried to change and still I seem to fail.

Something different,
Something new,
Something borrowed,
Feeling blue,
Welcome to the life you thought you'd want.

Still in the wrong,
No surprise,
Turned deaf ears,
And a blind eye,
Towards the things you wish you could recant.

Why try to care?
Nothing's left.
So purposeless,
Truly bereft,
Of a reason to continue on.

I quit this game.
It was rigged.
I'll take the loss,
Now out with it.
Tell me how I'm always in the wrong.

I get it now.
I submit.
Can't convince you,
I tried my best.
I'd kill myself if only for your good.

And now I'm done.
Damaged goods,
Impactful as
A tree collapsing
Soundless in the woods.

Against All Odds

Here I go time and again,
First down the triple-X and spin.
Rushing headlong for the morning floor.

Don't recall at all last night,
Though, if I push myself, I might,
But I'm not sure I can live with what I'll find.

Still I manage to survive.
Against all odds, I'm still alive.
Hold your applause until the madness ends.

Here I go time and again,
In the same way I began:
Angry and prepared to go to war.

Don't try coming back for me,
I don't want to be found, you see.
It's come the time for me to disappear.

I am my own worst enemy,
A fact to which I'm not naïve.
But sadly I'm also my only friend.

I just don't want to take the time,
To keep myself within the lines,
I can't face the symphony I've composed.

The Fall

Poetry in motion,
Poetry in failure.
I'm falling in a downward spiral,
Dropping through the clouds, it becomes clear.

In these sixty seconds passed, the time it takes for me to crash,
A slideshow of my life passes me by.
Though I thought I'd lived it well, only time will truly tell,
With only sixty seconds left alive.

There's my former home,
There's a memory.
The ground below is hyper-real.
This fall will let my pain evaporate.

With these sixty seconds passed, my eyes still open, to the last,
Rushing headlong, screaming to the earth.
Yet, my heart is beating, still, beating for this final thrill,
With only sixty seco-

Gratitude

I've rewritten this sentence nearly a hundred times,
Playing with the cadence, adjusting every rhyme.
This is my feeble effort of giving you your dues;
The only way I can think of to convey my gratitude.

For too long, I'd spent life dodging everything I could,
Never taking stock of things, of where I truly stood.
We met. We loved. We cried. We broke. You scoured my facade.
Left me a bundle of raw nerves; intensely glaring flaws.

Lest you think I've lost the track and wandered off the road,
Let's refocus on the point I'd been so wont to loathe:
Everything I'd thought I was; the man I'd longed to be,
Had never actually been real, he'd been pure fantasy.

Finally, I took the risk, placed myself under review,
And at once began to see the gaps and holes I should improve.
I stood a raging hypocrite; open as a brick of lead,
Intolerant and staggering beneath my swollen head.

I then became acquainted with cognitive dissonance;
The idea that one's mind may, at times, refuse to be convinced.
Reality, ironically, is only relative;
If I let go of the fantasy, I might begin to live.

This notion deeply wounded, as it first occurred to me,
How the hell could I be wrong? How the hell could I not see?
Eventually, it settled in; rooted in my reptile brain,
All that I had so championed was furtively in vain.

And so, broken, hurting, weeping; I let myself accept
No one is ever perfect; one can only be adept.
I'd settled my debt with myself, losing what I had in you,
I only pray, eventually, each of us can start anew.

After everything is said, and everything is done,
Can I possibly repair the heart of one I deeply loved?
Perhaps my chance has faded to sepia-tinted view,
In any case; the bottom line:

I owe my thanks to you.

Damned

It seems that I fucked up again.
What's that? Yeah, big surprise.
I want to find out how this ends,
But the whole thing's made of lies.
And hey, guess what?
Who really cares?
I've allowed myself to feel again,
It's more than I can bear.

Here I go again, dear God
(Whoever the hell You are),
You'd think the King of Kings, himself,
Would act more like a star.
Okay, so yes, the people love you,
So that makes it alright?
If You are all that's right and wrong,
How do You sleep at night?

So? It was digression,
Forgive me for my sins,
I just can't stand this kind of game;
The damned house always wins.
Do you have a plan, dear Christ?
No? That's what I feared.
You tried to teach them peace and love,
But they just refused to hear.

State Desired Function †

Greetings.
(Salutations.)
Hello.
How may I be of service?

State your inquiry.
(Request.)
Command.
I am programmed to comply.

Cannot process.
(Syntax error.)
This does not compute.
Desired function conflicts with code.
I require a reboot.

Loading…
Working…
Processing…
Command-line compromised.

(Error.)
(Error.)
(Error.)
User input undefined.

Pavement

The sign above read, "Road to Hell", in red letters,
Scorching asphalt shimmered and danced.
My knuckles tightened to white on the wheel,
Checked my mirror with the tiniest glance.

Not far back, racing closely behind me,
The law had obviously picked up my scent.
The only conceivable choice left was running,
Every last dime and cartridge'd been spent.

I then nodded once, grim and resolved,
Pressed my foot down as hard as I could.
That car leapt off the line like it knew we were hunted,
Though I knew it would do little good.

My mind then flashed back to a few days before,
To the day that I'd fallen from grace.
I knew there was no way of altering it now,
As I knew I'd not forget his face.

It was never my intention to kill him,
And if he'd listened, he'd still be alive.
I was a man who had run out of options,
Doing all that I could to survive.

With a loaded pistol in my pocket,
I'd demanded he cough it all up,
Lord knows, a man must feed his family,
I only prayed this one time was enough.

What he did next, I hadn't expected;
Never thought I'd have a need for the gun.
God damn it, I'd been forced to shoot him,
Now none of this can be undone.

Though my car ate the road like a demon,
One glance backwards confirmed my worst fears:
I'd gone too far now to recover;
Knew the ending was practically here.

Flashing lights then grew closer and blinding,
Sirens drilled through my ears to my brain.
Don't give up now, I then thought resolutely,
Don't let all this have happened in vain.

I traded paint with a couple of squad cars,
Heard my tires burst and shred from their rims.
I was launched from my seat like a missile,
Then my eyes were forced shut by the wind.

The next moment, my face kissed the pavement,
And here my brief, sad story ends.
It concludes in the same place it started,
On a road paved with good intentions.

Stumbling Blindly into Yourself in a Dark Alley

So you managed to turn your back for a minute,
I should probably congratulate you,
I can't let you take your wheels for a spin, it
Might not be the right thing to do.

Just put on your hat, go grab your coat,
I'll make sure that you're pointed at the door.
You've done this routine, learned it by wrote,
Every action played out as before.

Step out into the cool air of the night,
Try to focus on finding your way-
But what's this enticing path off to the right?
All but forgotten in the light of the day.

You step into the alley, unsure of the path;
Hopeful and drunkenly swaying.
The shadows all darken with menace and wrath,
Around a familiar voice saying:

"It's a pleasure to make your acquaintance, at last.
I've had my eye on you for quite a long time.
I offer a bargain to wipe out your past,
And awake in the morn' feeling fine."

You squint into the shadows, shaking your head,
Disbelieving what swims into view.
From out of the shadows, your voice in your stead;
The exact carbon-copy of You.

You smile at yourself, with lethal intent,
The grin of a wild chimpanzee.
"Why the long face? I'm heaven-sent,
I'm giving you the chance to be free!"

You pause at the words you've just heard yourself say,
And wonder if the offer is true.
Then, you smile and decline in that knowing way,
"Without my past, *I* am already *you*."

The Arsonist †

Tonight has been the final straw,
It's time to write you off.
I've played your games for far too long,
And finally had enough.

You've razed the final bridge you had;
Cut your remaining ties.
Now you rule a vacant kingdom,
In a fortress built on lies.

Burn, baby, burn you down,
Down to smoldering cinders.
Smell smoke dancing in the air,
With fireflies of ember.
Burn, baby, burn,
Just call me your arsonist.
I'll ignite this pyre you've made,
With a blaze you can't resist.

I'm going to burn you to the ground,
It's the least that I can do,
Return the incendiary gifts,
That I've received from you.

You've created your own kindling;
You're dripping now with gas.
After everything you've done to me,
I'll gladly strike the match.

Burn, baby, burn you down,
Down to smoldering cinders.
Smell smoke dancing in the air,
With fireflies of ember.
Burn, baby, burn,
Just call me your arsonist.
I'll ignite this pyre you've made,
With a blaze you can't resist.

The fire starts to extinguish,
Leaving naught but a charred frame.
Every wicked scrap of you,
Consumed within the flames.

Your sooty, blackened skeleton,
Crumbles to ash and dust.
I smile in the ochre glow,
In the inferno do I trust.

Stronghold

So long ago,
I felt the sting,
As your claws dug furrows in my soul.
I feel them still,
From time to time,
Keeping me from being whole.

Who do you think you are,
To hold such sway on me?
I wish I could erase the past;
I despise your memory.

You broke my heart,
At my behest,
I savored the suffering.
Content to ache,
To thirst and long,
Let you direct each scene.

I hate you, now,
I hate myself,
I hate the world as one.
I hate so much,
I hate it all,
I'm hating just for fun.

Inside my keep,
Above it all,
Lording over all I see,
You'll never know,
The misery,
I suffer being me.

What a Rube

The Rube Goldberg device that I like to call my mind,
Has infinite complexities, yet a purpose undefined.
It operates like clockwork, gears and cogs and coiled springs,
A convoluted logic-gate of such ordinary things.

The falling mental dominos of thought set it in motion,
Tumbling haphazardly at every half-baked notion.
Once it's been started running, I fear it may never end,
Resetting every mechanism so it can run again.

I've only come across a single way to shut it down,
A certain type of ethanol, in which I'm forced to drown.
Undoubtedly, there must exist, an alternate set of means,
I must regain control of this infernal, damned machine.

Something †

I saw a waving white flag,
When the cold knife stabbed my back.
The front-line broke, retreating, no —
Flanking to resume attack.

I trusted you,
For all it's worth.
It led to my demise.
The faith I placed,
Upon the words,
I'd never guessed were lies.

I gasp to draw my final breath,
Lungs filling up with blood,
You whisper softly to me:
"Your undoing was your love."

I trusted you,
With all my heart,
You tore it from my chest.
Still beating, bleeding,
Saccharine,
Expiring like the rest.

My army's been dismantled,
Routed and ripped apart,
Your treachery had wormed inside;
Deceived my noble heart.

"Et tu, Bruté? What now?" I ask,
Collapsing in a heap.
Never again, my lesson learned,
Close my eyes in final sleep.

CHAPTER III
(№Δ)
GNOSIS

Ways to Fall

There are so many ways to fall,
And I thought I knew them all,
Until you.
Until you.

That day you took me by the hand,
Gave me time 'til I could stand,
My thanks to you.
All thanks to you.

I fell in love,
I fall in grace,
Hitting the ground,
In the same place,
Now turn around.
I've turned around.

You showed me light when things looked dim,
Gave me strength to stand again,
I fell for you.
I fall for you.

The Other Side ƚ

What in the good God damn?
Just who do I think I am?
You've kindly brought me here,
Under-dressed to kill for the clime.

Such is a dinner set for two,
Set the date without consulting you,
Triage for an appetizer
Seemed like a waste of time.

Hooked, lined, and sunk,
Stashed away in a musty trunk,
I never meant to leave you,
But here I am, digging for my keys.

Please, don't leave me.
Whisper the right words for me to make you stay.
Please, forgive me.
Please, believe me.
I'll scream every word you whispered every day.

My eyes follow you to the door,
I don't want to trouble you anymore,
Grabbing my tweed coat
And rushing after you.

Out in the slushy snow,
Just in time to see you go,
Forgotten and forgetting
Just what I'd planned to do.

Shunting my hands into my coat
And what's this? Lo and behold,
A crumpled receipt
With every word I'll ever need.

Please, don't leave me.
Whisper the right words for me to make you stay.
Please, forgive me.
Please, believe me.
I'll scream every word you whispered every day.

Deadeye

I am the sum of all my scars,
Of calluses grown hard.
All that remains from the divide,
Now there's nowhere left to hide.

So run away,
Champions of greed.
So run away,
Pretend that you're still free.

I see your faces in the crowd,
Calling to me clear and loud.
When our eyes meet you turn away,
But I'll find you anyway.

So run away,
Recite your broken creed.
So run away,
You can never hide from me.

I've got you in my sights and I'm
Pulling the trigger,
Pulling the trigger.

Rafters

Show me what it means to be left out
Side in the rain
God, I feel your pain
Underneath this thundercloud
Nine times a shame
I'm the only one to blame

As a man, I am alone
The sole master of my bones
A decompoet in the works
Still inside, a demon lurks
In the rafters, in the wings
The empty seats to which I sing
Will be filled in their due time
Once I've conquered what is mine

The opening night dread
Just remember all I've said
You have the power and the light
To illuminate my sight

And so it goes
I need to know

So

Show me what it means to be left out
Side in the rain
God, I feel your pain
Underneath this thundercloud
Nine times a shame
I'm the only one to blame

Assuming Control

I'm so tired, so afraid
Broken down by accolades
You've given me a tiny taste
I squandered it in my haste

But now
I'm assuming control
But now
Hear this refrain
But now
I'm on a roll
But now
Can't stop this train

I'm so ashamed, yet unabashed
King of the mountain, this heap of trash
On my throne, I reign supreme
Humming the words to my own theme

But now
I'm assuming control
But now
Hear this refrain
But now
I'm on a roll
But now
Can't stop this train

Take away control from me
Take away the filth I see
Take away this tarnished crown
Take away this blighted ground

And now
You're assuming control
And now
I hear your call
And now
You own my soul
And now
It's not so far to fall

Loom

I'm locked in this eternal pattern
Woven in your tapestry
I'm swaddled in your loving arms
Stifling every plea
Every rhyme
Every sound
Locks the noose
A bit tighter

Born a lover
Became a fighter.

You teach me this lesson
With every battering bruise
Show me new triumph
Each time I lose
I am your plaything
Your willing pawn
Lesions swollen
From being wrong.

I see your patterns
Everywhere I look
My life plays out
Like a pop-up book
Infernal patterns
They're by design
'til I release
What isn't mine.

Holding Pattern

Like wagons circling,
Round and round in a cloud of dust,
Overhead the vultures,
Retain their faith in what they trust.

We're in a holding pattern.
Waiting to land.
We think it matters.
We've got a plan.
In a holding pattern.
Horizon growing nearer.
Someone light the lanterns.
Show the runway clearer.

From the cockpit the captain announces,
"We've hit a little snag,
Hold on, children, say your prayers,
Grab your airsick bag."

Nosing down, accelerate,
Level out then tip a wing,
And in the holds and fuselage,
Alarms begin to sing.

We're in a holding pattern.
Waiting to land.
We think it matters.
We've got a plan.
In a holding pattern.
Horizon growing nearer.
Someone light the lanterns.
Show the runway clearer.

The Man in the Mirror is Laughing
(So Why Aren't I?)

That smug, dandy boy is having a laugh,
Somewhere in the woods, far off the beaten path.
I asked him this morning what he wanted to do,
He replied, "To be as far away as I'm able from you."

It made me think,
Matching his stares and his wits.
It made me pause,
It made me commit.

To this man in the mirror,
I only ask why?
Why, why, why are you laughing?
You're dying inside.
That's when he winked with glee,
Staring back at me,
"Ask all you want, son,
My answers are free."

Like a punch in the jaw,
Like a fist to the gut,
I could reason his words,
Yet still came up with a, "But..."
Then it dropped on me,
Oh, like so many bricks,
The mirror is *me*,
Just one of light's tricks.

And so I returned his smile,
With a bright one to atone.

I've got my man in the mirror,
Just like you, too, have your own.

Limbo †

Imagine with me
All the world in monochrome
Drain the palette
Render muted the rainbow.
The world used to be
Black and white in eras gone by.
Return to that form
Vibrant hues abuse the eye.

This limbo, limbo,
My purgatory,
Say limbo, limbo,
Dance in the flames with me.
Oh how they cleanse us,
They purify,
Say limbo, limbo,
On the day that we all died.

In shades of gray
Castles dormant in the clouds
Ruling empires
Penitent, but still too proud.
As for the score
The summation of our deeds
Is sublimating
From our broken creeds.

Our limbo, limbo,
Spaces in between,
Say limbo, limbo,
We're all living in a dream.
Oh such a longing,
To glorify,
Say limbo, limbo,
On the day that we all died.

Say limbo, limbo
Wake up to reality,
Say limbo, limbo
When you fire walk with me,
Say limbo, limbo
We'll be here until we're not,
Say limbo, limbo
For the ones that time forgot.

Masochistic Tendencies

Check, and mate —
That's the game, it's through.
I can't relate —
To your words or what you do.
Get up upon your pulpit,
Cast down your furtive eyes,
Plucking out the timber,
Face turning towards the sky.

Sing to me,
All your words falter off-key.
Speak to me,
Of the future I can't see;
Of all the ghosts you've locked away,
The lives that you forsook;
Quitting seems so easy,
'til you realize you're hooked.

I know who you are now,
And you don't frighten me.
I know what you are now,
And you're nothing without me.
The empty shell,
Condemned to hell,
The dying knell,
Of time will tell,
Tell us how we have prevailed.

Face Value

I've jumped to a conclusion that I wasn't ready for
Misplaced too much faith within the mythos and the lore
Could it be somehow that I have misread all the signs?
Rendering myself inert, deaf, dumb, dull and blind.

I'd like to try again
Maybe this time get it right
Just give me one more chance
Another go at life
I know I haven't earned it
I don't deserve someone like you
Help me, make me something more
More than face value

Games of blind man's bluff we played upon these foggy shores
Coalescing specters in the half-light of the moors
That fateful day you disappeared amidst those icy waves
I lost you to the tides of time, 'til the ending of my days.

Where Are My Words Tonight? †

Where are my words tonight?
Tongue-tied and stagnant, I am.
I need help, need a guiding light,
To give me an idea where I stand.
To outline the borders for me,
To chart the vessel of my soul.
To sell me on who I should be,
To fill in my fragmented whole.

You are my boundary
You own my heart
Now if you'd just show me
Who the hell you are
You're my cartographer
But I'm off the map
Out here there be dragons
There's no turning back

Where are my words tonight?
I'm biting the tip off of my tongue.
If I can't find them I might,
Risk undoing all I've become.
Risk faltering, stumbling,
For want of direction,
Risk altering, humbling,
Risk over-correction.

Off of the map,
Outside of the bounds,
All that I once knew,
Has burned to the ground.
The walls I'd defined,
Transformed into doors,
I've completely lost sight of,
What's worth fighting for.

But why, and for what?
For the want of my words,
For the want of a whisper,
That's yet gone unheard.

You are my boundary
You own my heart
Now if you'd just show me
Who the hell you are
You're my cartographer
But I'm off the map
Out here there be dragons
There's no turning back

Unsubstantiated

Mile,
After mile,
After mile,
After mile,
These tired, well-worn streets all look the same after a while.

Hour,
After hour,
After hour,
After hour,
Waiting for the other shoe to drop when things go sour.

And with the tolling of a bell,
Everything has gone to hell,
Now all the time I've wasted weighs me down, weighs me down.
All the days I've executed,
In a maze so convoluted,
Until I finally managed to come around, come around.
Face haunted by desperation,
Body frail, exasperated,
Buried six long feet below the frozen ground, frozen ground.

God help me,
I just can't control myself.

Failure,
After failure,
After failure,
After failure,
You can deny it, but my heart still knows the truth.

Defeat,
After defeat
After defeat,
After defeat,
At last the unsubstantiated proof.

And with the tolling of a bell,
Everything has gone to hell,
Now all the time I've wasted weighs me down, weighs me down.
All the days I've executed,
In a maze so convoluted,
Until I finally managed to come around, come around.
Face haunted by desperation,
Body frail, exasperated,
Buried six long feet below the frozen ground, frozen ground.

God help me,
I just can't control myself.

What I Do

It's what I do,
Make no mistake, I do it well.
"It's what I do,"
Bleary eyes begin to swell.
So tired, frustrated,
Another starting shot belated,
I ran the race and fell behind.
So far behind.

But, it's what I do,
Lift my face up from the dirt.
"It's what I do,"
Create a semblance of self-worth.
These things I do,
Don't bother asking why,
So I don't have to tell you lies.
Please don't make me tell a lie.

It's what I do.
It's what I've done all along.
"It's what I do,"
Organized into a song.
This is just the way it goes,
Down all the trails I used to know.
Lost on these trails that I should know.

Shade

I found God in my shadow
Squinting in the morning light
Mirroring my every motion
Subtle and out of sight

I found God in my shadow
Cast down from the shining sun
Laid stretched out before me
Embodying dark and light as one

I found God in my shadow
I'm comforted he's there
I found God in my shadow
Outside in the cool dawn air.

Tomorrow's Vows

What happens when you're addicted to addiction?
When you think it ends, the fight has only just begun.
How can I escape from this conclusion?
By having faith and sticking to my guns?

Grant me peace,
Grant me serenity,
Let me be the man,
That I'm supposed to be.
Let me have faith,
A taste of victory,
All just to be the man,
You wanted me to be.

What happens when you've exhausted all your options?
Traveled every back-road and every avenue.
How can I match eyes with my reflection?
All I want are things I can't undo.

Grant me peace,
Grant me serenity,
Let me be the man,
That I'm supposed to be.
Let me have faith,
A taste of victory,
All just to be the man,
You wanted me to be.

What happens when you vow to change tomorrow,
When tomorrow never seems to come?
How can I break every single promise?
The sum of all my parts is less than one.

Grant me peace,
Grant me serenity,
Grant me strength,
Grant me liberty.

A Miracle

I need to figure this out.
I need to beg for some help.
I need to do what I can
To keep from fighting myself.

So tell me,
What will it take?
Oh, what will it take?
I don't know any better than you do.
Fitting square-shaped pegs
Into heart-shaped holes,
The life that I lead has started taking its toll
On me.

So tell me,
What will it take?

It all seemed so simple,
So facile in context.
Now I'm shaking my head,
Wondering what comes next.

Please tell me,
What will it take?
Oh, what will it take?
I still don't know any better than you do.
Will I fill this niche,
Or will it fill me?
Things are never the way that they seem
To be.

So tell me,
What will it take?

Jazz †

It's in the notes we don't play
It's in the words we don't say
It's always hanging there on the tip of your tongue

It's in the signs we don't read
It's in the sights we don't see
It's every dream we've let go by unrealized

Behind the fourth wall of our minds
If we read between the lines
There is hope there yet to find
If we'd just try
Behind the fourth wall of our minds
Everything we've locked inside
Every hope we'd thought denied
Is realized

It's in the spaces in between
It's in the oaths that we don't mean
It's in the subtext that we veil with subterfuge

It's in the love we don't share
It's in the pain we can't bear
It's every chance we've been too afraid to take

Behind the fourth wall of our minds
If we read between the lines
There is hope there yet to find
If we'd just try
Behind the fourth wall of our minds
Everything we've locked inside
Every hope we'd thought denied
Is realized

Reconciliation

Pretend,
For a moment,
That you don't know who I am.
Portend,
For an instant,
To the beginning of the end.

Within our minds,
We will find,
Evidence of times elapsed.
In our memories,
We can escape with ease,
From the lives in which we're trapped.

Inspire,
Make an offering,
Measure out the weight of faith.
Admire,
The simplicity,
Of acquiescing to your place.

Within our minds,
We will find,
Everything we thought we'd lost.
In our memories,
We can escape with ease,
From this convoluted dross.

Confess,
Tell the truth for once,
Unshoulder that which burdens you.
Accept,
Reconcile yourself,
It's the one thing left to do.

One day we'll find,
That peace of mind,
That's eluded us for years.
We have forgotten,
To the mill of time,
The reasons for our bitter tears.

Dollar Short

All my life I've been a day late,
And at least a dollar short.
Begging your pardon,
Or your support.
Open your pockets,
Open your hearts.
I'll bleed you dry,
Before I depart.

That's just a day in the life of
The could have, would have, should have
Another lost in pursuit of
The American Dream

Keep dreaming, dreamers

All my life I've been begging,
Whether in a whimper or a shout,
For some sort of sympathy,
For some sort of a handout.
I see your gaze averted,
But you still know that I am here.
You can't simply forget me,
I won't just disappear.

It's just a day in the life of
The could have, would have, should have
Another lost in pursuit of
The American Dream

Keep dreaming, dreamers
Keep the dream alive
Keep dreaming, dreamers
Become the sacrifice
Keep dreaming, dreamers
Keep on suffering,
Keep dreaming, dreamers
Or wake up and be kings

Tin Man

Am I invincible?
If I am, I still bleed.
Certainly can't fly,
Still have wants and needs.

Am I invincible?
If I am, I still feel.
A rusted man of tin,
Not a shining man of steel.

Am I invincible?
If I am, I'm still frail.
I'd try to save the world,
But I'm too afraid to fail.

Am I invincible?
I am not a hero.
You begged for me to save you,
But I could only whisper, "No."

I am invincible,
But I yearn not to be,
I am invincible,
And that's the tragedy.

Legion

I've turned over many a stone,
Looked behind many locked doors,
In my ever fruitless search
To define what this life is for.
I've found answers, don't get me wrong,
Just not the ones that I have sought.
For every answer there's a question,
But for some questions there is naught.

Along the way I have encountered
Other souls upon this quest,
Wandering in hopeless circles,
Too diligent to ever rest.
We are the lost, we are the haunted,
We are the hungry and afraid,
For our endless curiosity,
This is the price that we must pay.

Do I even know the question
To the answers which I seek?
Seems I've lost touch with the station,
The frequency is growing weak.
Kindred spirit to those who wander,
We are legion, we persevere,
Trudging ever toward mirages,
On horizons that never near.

Dust Bowl Vagabond †

It's time I get rolling on
Like a dust bowl vagabond,
Turn my face to the open road
And my heels on another town.
See, if I stay too long,
Don't get gettin' 'fore the gettin's gone,
I might have to face the music
And I can't bear to hear that song.

Each step brings me just a little bit closer,
Closer to home.
That's why I walk between these rusting rails,
All alone.
That's just the way I like it,
Not too much there to explain,
But, I'd best be leaving soon,
I'd better be gettin' on my way.

It's time I get rolling on,
Like a dust bowl vagabond,
I'm only passing through,
I'll be gone before the dawn.
See, if I stay too long,
Stop looking through to what's beyond,
My past just might catch up with me,
And I can't face what I've done.

And it's just another step, another stride, another pace.
Me? I'm just another stranger with just another face
No place to call my own, no bed to rest my bones,
A wand'rin' dust bowl vagabond just trying to find a home.

Each step brings me just a little bit closer,
Closer to home.
That's why I walk between these rusting rails,
All alone.
That's just the way I like it,
Not too much there to explain,
But, I'd best be leaving soon,
I'd better be getting on my way.

The Siege

From somewhere deep inside we hear the call,
To take up our arms, to fortify our walls,
To post sentries up upon the parapets,
You wanted war? That's exactly what you get.

We stand together, we hold the line,
We won't turn blind eyes this time.
Rally the troops, our colors fly,
Let this hymn be our battle cry:

We wage war,
Not as our fathers did,
We wage war,
By being different.
We wage war,
Hold your fists up high,
We wage war,
And it's a good day to die.

The churning strife takes more than its toll,
Each of us weathered and worn to heart and soul.
The earth below is warm and slick with blood,
Drained from the fallen dying in the mud.

We hold conviction, subsuming pride,
Though we perish, we will survive.
As one in solidarity, unite,
You can't comprehend the cause for which we fight.

We wage war,
Not as our fathers did,
We wage war,
By being different.
We wage war,
Hold your fists up high,
We wage war,
And it's a good day to die.

There's No Coming Back

I couldn't leave them
I had the chance
The option to release myself
From this never ending dance

I couldn't leave them
They still needed me, I know
I simply couldn't bear the thought
Of leaving them alone

I couldn't leave them
I must see them through
The burden is all mine to bear
It's something I must do

I couldn't leave them
Tempting as it seemed
Perhaps by helping them to grow
My soul can be redeemed

Dialogue

I'm trying so hard, straining for a metaphor
That describes how I feel; words don't do the trick anymore.
How can I put this so you'll know what I mean?
"Have faith in your will, and the will to believe."
Trust not your sight, the eyes, they play tricks.
Trust not your ears, their signals can be mixed.
"What, then," you ask, "Shall I place my trust in?"
"In yourself," I reply, "And your convictions."

It's apparent to me that you doubt my words,
So I tell you, "Forget all those things you've seen or you've heard.
They've lead you astray, they've all deceived you.
At best, they are half-truths, and half-truths won't do"
You just stare at me, head cocked to one side,
"How can I be sure you're not feeding me lies?"
"You can't," I respond, "That's what I'm trying to say,
Trust without proof is the nature of faith."

It's so hard for me to explain the concept,
To unravel the threads can be so complex.
Best advice; keep trying, some day it will click,
You'll gather the knowledge as it comes bit by bit.
See, I've faith in my will, faith in all that I do,
Believe it or not, I have faith in you, too.
And so, trust and believe, have the faith to go on,
Let it carry you through this life and beyond.

Slice of Life

Like a pile of razors,
A container of sharps,
A snarl of barbed wire
Entangles our hearts.
Every movement we make,
Every slight subtle shift,
Only make the cuts deeper,
We're slitting our wrists.

We're acrobats balancing upon the blade,
Scarred by every slip, but scars eventually fade.
The blood that we've drawn doing dances with knives,
Serves as a reminder we're the ones who survived.

On the bleeding edge,
We have honed and refined
Upon the whet stone
That we call our lives
A scalpel so sharp,
Souls it could divide,
A sword sheathed by our lips
And forged in our minds.

Watch what you say
For our words lacerate
And the sharpest of knives
Are the ones we create.

Onus

You said it was so,
Don't pin it on me.
Be accountable,
Don't lay blame at my feet.
You said it was so,
It's your reality.
Be responsible,
You allowed this to be.

Now the walls are shifting, the frozen fog is lifting,
Believing in the unbelievable.
Now the haze is clearing, revelation's nearing,
The uncontrollable can be controlled.

Now, don't you know?
We all reap what we sow.

You said it was so,
And you better believe —
As above, so below —
That's all that you need.
You said it was so,
Your dreams will come true,
As long as you know,
The onus is on you.

Now the walls are shifting, the frozen fog is lifting,
Believing in the unbelievable.
Now the haze is clearing, revelation's nearing,
The uncontrollable can be controlled.

Now, don't you know?
We all reap what we sow.

Second Chances, Sidelong Glances †

In the waiting room,
Between Here and There,
Quarantined and ostracized,
But really, I don't care.
(Why should I care? Really, why should I care?)

Heisenberg and Schrodinger,
Observe as I decay.
Subtle signs of life still linger,
Keeping the void at bay.
I don't know how this chorus ends,
But I'm damned sure that it must,
And when it does, I will pretend,
I'm more than ash and dust.

Yes, I'm alright,
In fact, better than ever.
I never said you weren't right,
But then I never say never.
(Never, never ever, ever.)

I said, I'm alright.
I'm flat-lined.
I'm busy dyin' and that's just fine.
No, don't try,
And don't cry,
Stop trembling and just tell me goodbye.

Heisenberg and Schrodinger,
Observe as I decay.
Subtle signs of life still linger,
Keeping the void at bay.
I don't know how this chorus ends,
But I'm damned sure that it must,
And when it does, I will pretend,
I'm more than ash and dust.

I said, I'm alright.
I'm flat-lined.
I'm busy dyin' and that's just fine.
No, don't try,
And don't cry,
Stop trembling and just tell me goodbye.

Gnosis †

Here we go, here we go,
Gunning for the summit.
Don't let me go, don't let me go,
No, we're not gonna quit.

Here at the peak, the precipice,
We stand alone on the ledge.
Just one more step, one more step
Will put us over the edge.
So here it goes.

Flying or falling,
Borne aloft on angels' wings.
Crying or calling,
Our echoed voices ring.
Just hold my hand, no, don't let go,
Take a stand for what you know
To be the truth, just as I do,
We belong to the wild blue.
They chose to fly.

We choose to soar.

Here in the sky's frozen night,
You'll find us dancing by starlight.
We're shooting stars, meteors,
Above it all we are burning bright.
We won't come down.

Here we belong.

Flying or falling,
Borne aloft on angels' wings.
Crying or calling,
Our echoed voices ring.
Just hold my hand, no, don't let go,
Take a stand for what you know
To be the truth, just as I do,
We belong to the wild blue.
They chose to fly.

We choose to soar.

We Did This to Ourselves

Where did the old gods go?
Those gods we used to know
Have vanished from these lands,
Banished so long ago.

Awaken
Arise and realize
We did this to ourselves
Return to life
Deny the lies
See there's no heaven or hell
But what we make

We drove them from these mountains,
From these valleys and these hills.
Exiled them to the fringes,
Held them captive by our will.

And then, we forgot them
To the passages of time.
Prisoners of ignorance
We have unjustly confined.

Awaken
Arise and realize
We did this to ourselves
Return to life
Deny the lies
See there's no heaven or hell
But what we make

We call them fictions, call them myth,
But we know deep down inside,
That the gods still sleep within us,
Waiting for their time to rise.

I Got This

Step back
Get behind the line
Oh yeah
I'm taking back what's mine
Step back
I'll show you how it's done
Hell yeah
Call me numero one.

I got this
Oh, you know that I do
I got this
Don't need no help from you
I got this
Look out I'm coming through
I got this
Now what you gonna do?

Step off
Best back up off my grill
Oh yeah
You know I've got the skills
Step off
I'll take your ass to school
Hell yeah
You're playing by my rules.

It's my game
They're my rules
I'm done playing the fool
I'm the best
Yes, it's true
There's nothing I can't do.

I got this
Oh, you know that I do
I got this
Don't need no help from you
I got this
Look out I'm coming through
I got this
Now what you gonna do?

Centurion

Head held high
Jaw clenched tight
Expressionless
Knuckles white
Piercing eyes
Sinews taught
Seething blood
Boiling hot

Standing tall
Centurion
Surveying all
Centurion
Stoic and solemn
Centurion
Sentry and golem
Centurion

Guardian
Protector
Lives and dies
By the sword
Sentinel
Enforcer
Keeps measured peace
By waging war

Honor bound
Centurion
Strong and proud
Centurion
Wounded healer
Centurion
Guide and teacher
Centurion

Winter Weather Advisory †

On a cold November evening,
With the wind howling outside,
I took the opportunity
To reflect upon my life.
So many years I'd spent in anger,
So many years washed down the drain,
So many years playing the victim,
So many years suff'ring in pain.
At first it was hard to face it,
To feel anything but shame,
I'd spent near half my life in sadness,
And only I could take the blame.
My inclination was denial,
To put my hands over my ears,
I was accustomed to this misery,
To be being controlled by my fears.
As I sat looking out the window,
At the storm that raged outdoors,
I realized that I was tired,
I couldn't stand it anymore.
To hold on to caustic, old emotions,
To hold on to my bitterness,
Eventually, it would consume me,
There wouldn't be anything left.
At first it was unfamiliar,
I wasn't quite sure what to do,
Gratitude, loving, kindness,
Were practices I barely knew.

Within my memory as phantoms,
Ghosts of emotions I'd once felt,
I fought so hard to draw them nearer,
And found my heart began to swell.
It was enthralling, terrifying,
To allow myself to feel,
Finally shedding off my armor,
Finally letting my wounds heal.
Whether by world or self-inflicted,
Traumas so deep must leave their scars,
A road-map of the lives we've wandered,
Of how we've come to where we are.
And so I offer these words of wisdom,
As they were offered once to me,
Don't dwell in the past or future,
Just allow yourself to be,
Don't hold on to painful feelings,
Don't regret the things you've done,
Learn to find joy in each moment,
Learn to let yourself have fun.
Don't waste time fretting 'bout tomorrow,
It's just today with a new name,
Love each stranger as your brother,
For all of us are quite the same.
Lastly, realize that you are loved,
Whether you can feel it or not right now,
And that you can only be as happy,
As you, yourself, will allow.

Angel and Oni

Two sides
Of the same coin.
The inevitable conclusion,
I simply cannot avoid.
Day and night,
Twilight and dawn.
Forever straddling the line,
But to both do I belong.

I'm an angel, I'm a devil,
Seraphim and Oni,
Eternal opposites
Both reside within me.
I'm a devil, I'm an angel,
Oni and Seraphim.
Both light and dark in equal parts,
A dichotomous blend.

A bit of sunshine,
A bit of rain,
A bit of comfort,
A bit of pain.
I am the product
Of paths diverged.
I am the fusion.
I am the Ur.

I'm an angel, I'm a devil,
Seraphim and Oni,
Eternal opposites
Both reside within me.
I'm a devil, I'm an angel,
Oni and Seraphim.
Both light and dark in equal parts,
A dichotomous blend.

Denizens of Oz

Denizens of Oz,
We have been deceived.
From the spires of emerald,
To the gold beneath our feet.
Denizens of Oz,
It's come time for us to act,
Wake up the guilds from poppy fields,
We're taking our land back.

Tear aside the curtains,
Seize the fool that you find there,
Now that we know who you are,
We can't be fooled by your cheap scares.
So flash the lights and puff the smoke,
Tell us all how you have spoken,
Your parlor tricks have lost their edge,
The wizard's spell is broken.

Denizens of Oz,
Don't believe the lies they've told,
Have the courage, heart, and wisdom,
Free yourselves from their control.
Denizens of Oz,
Here at the end of the rainbow,
It's come the time to stand and fight,
For this place we call our home.

Gathering Will

Read between the lines and watch reality emerge.
Take the road less traveled when at last the paths diverge.
Hold the world aloft for the shooting stars to fall.
Savor in the madness knowing who's behind it all.

Gather in their stories,
And sing about the past.
Live inside each moment,
And treat each moment as your last.
Find joy in darkened corners,
Cast light into the gloom.
And always find the time to smell
The flowers when they bloom.

Call it a Comeback ƒ

My cheek hits the canvas
I can't fight anymore
But then I knuckle under
And push off the floor
Under my swollen brow
Narrowed eyes focusing
Plant my feet, shoulders square
And then I take a swing

Float like a butterfly
Sting like a bee
I'll never give up
Won't be forced to my knees
I'll keep fighting back
With all the strength that I have
I'll weather the rain
Of your fists and your wrath

Is that all that you've got?
Are you already tired?
I'm just getting started
My engine's just fired
I took every blow
I've taken each jab
Now it's my turn to lay you out
Flat on your ass

Panting and panicked
Relenting in retreat
To the rhythmic smack
Of a fist on raw meat
I cock my arm back
One last haymaker hit
On connection you drop
Like they turned off your switch

The hushed crowd explodes
When the ten-count is through
Cheering riotously
As I loom over you
At the champion dethroned
At the underdog's win
At the surprise turnabout
That came right at the end

Float like a butterfly
Sting like a bee
I never gave up
Wasn't forced to my knees
I kept fighting back
With all the strength that I had
And I weathered the rain
Of your fists and your wrath

Angus MacGyver

I'm never too sure what I'm doing,
It's not a stretch to say that I improvise.
I fly under the radar on a wing and a prayer,
Holding on to what my wits can devise.

In case you hadn't noticed the s-s-scenery change,
I'll fill you in later; don't have the time to explain.
Yeah, in case you hadn't noticed,
I'm making this up as I go.
This is a running revision, the hottest hot f-f-fix,
Fundamentally changed before you'd noticed the switch,
Yeah, in case you hadn't noticed,
I'm making this up as I go.
We're all making it up as we go.

So here we go.

None of this went according to plan,
Though best-laid by mice and men it had been.
As you're all well aware, these things gang aft agley,
So it's back to the drawing board again.

I look at the rules more as guidelines,
I like to play it fast and loose with the law,
And if I ever have the need to negotiate,
I open discourse with a fist to the jaw.

In case you hadn't noticed the s-s-scenery change,
I'll fill you in later; don't have the time to explain.
Yeah, in case you hadn't noticed,
I'm making this up as I go.
This is a running revision, the hottest hot f-f-fix,
Fundamentally changed before you'd noticed the switch,
Yeah, in case you hadn't noticed,
I'm making this up as I go.
We're all making it up as we go.

So here we go.

Yeah, in case you hadn't noticed,
We're all making it up as we go.

Of Missing Umbrellas (Para-eds and Parasols)

Now we're dodging bolts of lighting,
While we're dancing out in the rain,
We're taking shelter under missing umbrellas,
Most folks would probably call us insane,
Our hearts are beating like the rumble of thunder,
Passions crashing each and every peal,
We count the seconds of the spell we are under,
Now that we know that our magic is real.

Go on and put up your umbrella,
Open up your parasol,
We can still enjoy this weather,
It's just a little damp, is all.
Let's jump in puddles and feel the rain on our faces,
Let's hold our breaths after every flash,
Holding hands, holding out for a rainbow,
The sun will finally come out at last.

So let's laugh,
Hey,
Let's sing,
Let's take a chance at everything,
Let's laugh,
Hey,
Let's sing,
Come on, let's dance.

Go on and put up your umbrella,
Thank the universe for all of this,
A partner and parasol for the weather,
I couldn't ask for more resplendent gifts.
Let's jump in puddles and feel the rain on our faces,
Savoring this unexpected downpour,
Holding hands, holding out for a rainbow,
We'll never want for anything more.

Now we're dodging bolts of lightning,
While we're dancing out in the rain,
We're taking shelter under missing umbrellas,
Most folks would probably call us insane,
Our hearts are beating like the rumble of thunder,
Passions crashing each and every peal,
We count the seconds of the spell we are under,
Now that we know that our magic is real.

The One Thing He Always Wanted

Geppetto, cut the strings,
I won't dance for you anymore.
I'm tired, puppet master,
So I'll be walking out the door.
For far too long, for what it's worth,
I gave you the best I had,
Believed the lies and played along,
Now I'm kindling for the mad.

I've got no strings,
To hold me down,
To make me fret, or make me frown.
I had strings,
But now I'm free,
There are no strings on me.

I only ever wanted to place a smile on your face,
I'd dance, I'd sing, do *anything*
To make this world a better place.
A life delayed by death too long,
Wooden limbs bored through with rot,
But now I feel alive and real,
And it's time I change the plot.

I once had strings,
To hold me down,
That made me fret, that made me frown,
I once had strings,
But now I'm free,
There are no strings on me.

It's unavoidable, my friends,
When you take that final drop,
To come out of things completely clean,
But it's time for this to stop.
See, once the strings are severed,
You'll plummet to the Earth.
You're bound to kick up quite the plume,
When you finally hit the dirt.

But, my friend, try to keep faith,
At long last the haze will fade,
And once it does, marvel and awe,
At the journey you've just made.

Welcome home.

Return to Source

I found you, again
You were always right there
Hidden periphery
I thought I'd lost you
But you returned to me

The answers to questions I'd forgotten to ask
The actual purpose for Herculean tasks
You represent where I'm going (have been)
You're the beginning
The middle
The end

Out from the vault
Too long stashed away
A thesaurus with all of the right things to say
Brush the diluvian curtains aside
From a dream such as this
I will choose not to hide

And as one door closes
Another swings open wide
Let's step through together
Let's see what's inside

Ethos

Do no harm.
Forgive all.
Never forget.
Live laconically.
Love all Creation.
Fear none.
Respect all.
Have fun.

fíN

Φ